# WEIRD NATURE

By Virginia Loh-Hagan

Disclaimer: This series focuses on the strangest of the strange. Have fun reading about strange people and things! But please do not try any of the antics in this book. Be safe and smart!

**45th Parallel Press**

Published in the United States of America by Cherry Lake Publishing
Ann Arbor, Michigan
www.cherrylakepublishing.com

Reading Adviser: Marla Conn MS, Ed., Literacy specialist, Read-Ability, Inc.
Book Designer: Melinda Millward

Photo Credits: © Department for International Development/http://www.flickr.com/ CC-BY-2.0, cover, 17; © Dizdnk/Shutter stock.com, 1; © Gekko Gallery/Shutterstock.com, 5; © rickredds/Shutterstock.com, 6; © CoolR/Shutterstock.com, 7; © Thawornnurak/Shutterstock.com, 8; © Waddell Images/Shutterstock.com, 9; ©Lightguard/iStockphoto, 10; © United States Coast Guard, 11; © Chad McDermott/Shutterstock.com, 12; © Thomas Wong/Shutterstock.com, 14; © Kristina D.C. Hoeppner / http://www.flickr.com/CC BY-SA 2.0, 15; © Asianet-Pakistan/Shutterstock.com, 16; © Thorsten Rust/Shutterstock.com, 18; © dangdumrong/Shutterstock.com, 19; © Rod Waddington/http://www.flickr.com/CC BY-SA 2.0, 20; © Ann Stryzhekin/ Shutterstock.com, 21; © Mark Moffett/ Minden Pictures/Newscom, 22; © Liz Glasco/Shutterstock.com, 24; © Sankei / Getty Images, 25; © Richair/Dreamstime.com, 26; © ASSOCIATED PRESS, 27; © VCG/Getty Images, 29; © fmajor/iStockphoto, 30

Graphic Element Credits: ©saki80/Shutterstock.com, back cover, front cover, multiple interior pages; ©queezz/Shutterstock. com, back cover, front cover, multiple interior pages; ©Ursa Major/Shutterstock.com, front cover, multiple interior pages; ©Zilu8/Shutterstock.com, multiple interior pages

**45th Parallel Press** is an imprint of Cherry Lake Publishing.

Library of Congress Cataloging-in-Publication Data

Names: Loh-Hagan, Virginia, author.
Title: Weird nature / by Virginia Loh-Hagan.
Description: Ann Arbor, MI : Cherry Lake Publishing, [2017] | Series: Stranger than fiction |
     Audience: Grades 7 to 8. | Includes bibliographical references and index.
Identifiers: LCCN 2017003161| ISBN 9781634728942 (hardcover) | ISBN 9781534100725 (pbk.) |
     ISBN 9781634729833 (pdf) | ISBN 9781534101616 (hosted ebook)
Subjects: LCSH: Nature–Miscellanea–Juvenile literature. | Curiosities and wonders–Juvenile literature. |
     Animals–Miscellanea–Juvenile literature.
Classification: LCC QH48 .L64 2017 | DDC 001.94–dc23
LC record available at https://lccn.loc.gov/2017003161

Printed in the United States of America
Corporate Graphics

## About the Author

Dr. Virginia Loh-Hagan is an author, university professor, former classroom teacher, and curriculum designer. She got rid of the nature in her backyard by building a pool. She lives in San Diego with her very tall husband and very naughty dogs. To learn more about her, visit www.virginialoh.com.

# Table of Contents

# Introduction

Nature is all around us. It's plants. It's animals. It's weather. It's oceans. It's **landforms**. Landforms include mountains and hills. They're anything formed by the earth.

Nature is amazing. It's beautiful. It gives people joy. It gives people life. It can also be mean. It can cause damage. It can hurt people.

There are many strange things in nature. Nature also does many strange things. Some things are stranger than others. They're so strange that they're hard to believe. They sound like fiction. But these stories are all true!

*Flora is plants. Fauna is animals.*

# chapter one

# Elephant Rock

Elephant Rock is a large stone. It's in Italy. It's beside a state road. It's right outside a big town. It looks like an elephant. Its trunk is turned upward. It's pointed at the road.

Elephant Rock was part of a bigger mountain. But it broke off. It rolled down the valley. It rolled along the road. It got stuck. Then, **erosion** occurred. Erosion is when nature slowly wears something down. Weather, wind, and water affect things. They changed the rock's shape.

Elephant Rock has openings and holes. The inside is made of caves. Symbols from the Stone Age are on the walls.

6

There are other elephant rocks around the world.

# chapter two

# Fire Rainbows

Fire rainbows are special. They're not made of fire. They're not rainbows. They're **optical** events. Optical means visual. They rarely happen. They need special conditions. It has to be summer. The sun has to be high in the sky. It has to be in a certain position. Fire rainbows are formed in developing clouds. They often form in thunderstorms. These clouds have water droplets that bend light. Sunlight enters the clouds' ice crystals. It has to enter at the perfect angle. This splits the colors.

*A fire rainbow is also called an ice halo.*

Fire rainbows are large. They have bright color bands. They have brilliant pastel colors. They look like flames.

# chapter three

# Bermuda Triangle

Something odd happened on December 5, 1945. Five U.S. Navy planes took off. They were on a mission. They flew over the Atlantic Ocean. They disappeared. This mystery inspired stories about the "Bermuda Triangle."

The area looks like a triangle. It's between Miami, Bermuda, and San Juan. Miami is in Florida. Bermuda is an island. San Juan is in Puerto Rico. It covers about 500,000 square miles (1.3 million square kilometers) of sea.

Many people, planes, and boats get lost in this area. About 20 boats and four planes are lost per year. They vanish without a

*The mission was known as Flight 19.*

trace. There are no bodies. There's no **wreckage**.
Wreckage is pieces from boats and planes.

The Bermuda Triangle has deep **trenches**. Trenches are holes. They're long and narrow. They're on the seafloor. Bodies and wreckage sink. They sink into these trenches.

The area is dangerous. It has sharp rocks. It has high waves. It has rough weather. It has strong **currents**. Currents are water flows.

The area affects **compasses**. Compasses are tools. They help people get from one place to another. The area makes directions unstable. This creates confusion. People lose their way.

*Dragon's Triangle is like the Bermuda Triangle. It's off Japan's east coast.*

# Explained by Science

How did the universe begin? Some scientists believe in "the big bang theory." Theory means an idea. Scientists learned that other solar systems move away from ours. Farther systems move at greater speeds. They move in all directions. It's like the systems are pushed by a force. This made scientists come up with the big bang theory. First, the universe was one hot, thick mass. Then, a big blast blew it up. This happened 10 billion to 20 billion years ago. Next, energy spread out. This all happened in less than a second. Last, stars and planets formed. Scientists think the universe keeps spreading out. But the movement is slower. It takes billions of years to move.

# chapter four

# Glowworm Caves

Waitomo Glowworm Caves are in New Zealand. Waitomo means "water hole." These caves formed 30 million years ago. Glowworms line the ceilings. They shine a bright light. The light is blue-green. The caves look magical.

The glowworms are **larvae**. They're the stage between eggs and adult flies. They're tiny. They spin silk nests. They start at the ceiling. They lower threads down. They catch fish.

People take boat rides. They travel on an underground river. They go 150 feet (46 meters) underground. They travel under

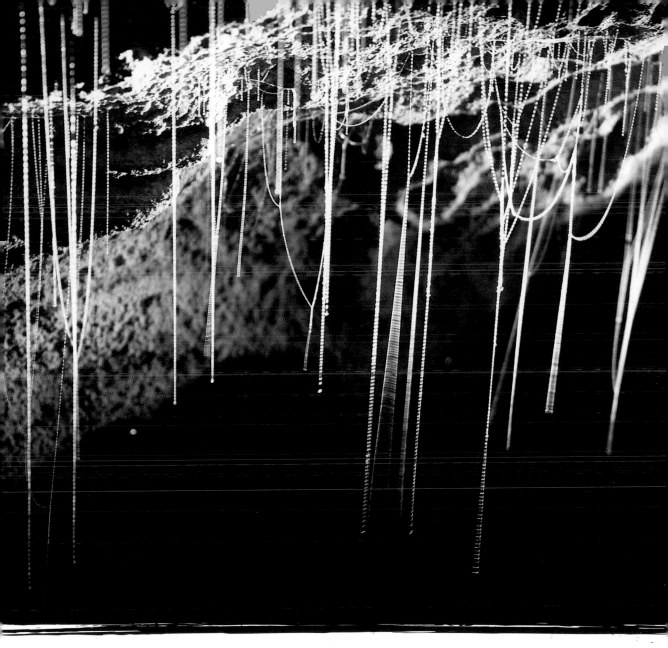

*These caves are part of a bigger cave system.*

the glowworms. They look up. They see thousands
of twinkling lights.

# chapter five

# Ghost Trees

Sindh is a village. It's in Pakistan. It was flooded. This happened in 2010. **Monsoons** hit the area. They're heavy rains with wind. They dropped 10 years of rainfall. They did this in a week. They filled the rivers. Rivers overflowed. They created pools all over the area.

Millions of spiders escaped the floods. They crawled into trees. They spun webs over the trees. The trees are in a farm field in Sindh. They look like ghosts. They look like **cocoons**. Cocoons are silky wraps.

*Almost 2,000 people died in the flood. But the spiders lived.*

The spiders are helping. Some mosquitoes carry sicknesses. Spiders eat the mosquitoes. Now there are fewer mosquitoes in Sindh.

# chapter six

# Koala Bears

Koala bears live in Australia. They live in trees. They eat poisonous leaves. They have special digestive systems. Their stomachs have **bacteria**. Bacteria are like bugs living in bodies. Koala bacteria fight poison.

But koala babies don't have bacteria. Moms help babies. Koalas eat a lot. They make special poop. It's called **pap**. It has a lot of bacteria. Babies eat this pap. They get the bacteria. The pap is runny and wet. It gets messy. Babies eat it for a month. This is how they get healthy. After eating pap, babies switch to eating leaves.

The bacteria in pap keeps koala bears alive.

# chapter seven

# Dragon Blood Trees

Dragon blood trees are in Socotra. Socotra is a group of islands. It's in the Arabian Sea. The trees look strange. Their treetops form crowns. They look like umbrellas. The shape helps the trees **survive**. Survive means to stay alive.

Socotra is **arid**. This means dry. There's little water. There's also little soil. The treetops are **densely** packed. Dense means thick. The crowns provide shade. They hold water in. This reduces **evaporation**. Evaporation is when water changes to a gas. The shade also helps **seedlings** grow. Seedlings are baby plants. They're under the crowns. These trees grow close together.

*Dragon blood trees usually flower in February.*

Dragon blood trees have red **sap**. Sap is tree juice. People thought the sap was special. It was thought to be dragon's blood. People want this sap. They use it as a **dye**. Dyes are colors. Some people use it as lipstick. It was also used to paint violins.

Most people use the sap for medicine. They use it to heal wounds. They use it to stop bleeding. They use it to cure pooping problems. They use it for fevers.

The trees have small berries. The berries start out green. Then, they turn black. When ripe, they turn orange-red. The berries make red juice. They make more dragon's blood.

*The sap from dragon blood trees has many uses.*

# Spotlight Biography

Steve Irwin was famous. He was the "Crocodile Hunter." He was Australian. He was a wildlife expert. He was killed by a stingray. His son was two years old when he died. His son is Robert Irwin. He looks like his father. He wants to be like his father. Robert Irwin said, "I'm keen to do everything he did." He works with animals. He cohosts his own show. His show is called *Wild But True*. Once, he fed a crocodile. He did this at age 12. He got too close. The crocodile snapped its jaws. Wes Mannion handles animals. He grabbed Irwin's shirt. He pulled him to safety. Irwin also takes pictures of wildlife. He won an award.

# chapter eight

# Red Tides

Red tides happen on the coast. They're not connected to tides. They happen at certain times of the year. Waters turn red. This is caused by **algae**. Algae are seaweed. Many algae appear. They bloom. They turn red or brown. Red tides happen when algae grow quickly in water. Algae form dense patches near the surface. This colors the water.

Red tides are pretty. But some algae are poisonous. They cause breathing problems. They kill animals that eat them. People have found beaches of dead animals. People can get sick if they eat infected animals.

*Red tides may be the basis of a Bible story.*
*The story says the waters turned to blood.*

# chapter nine

# Hole Punch Cloud

People in California saw a big hole in the sky. They thought they saw an alien spaceship. But they saw a hole punch cloud.

Clouds are made of water droplets. Sometimes, part of a cloud falls out. This leaves behind a hole. The hole is caused by a **localized** snowstorm. Localized means collected in one place. The hole is shaped like a circle.

Temperatures drop in the hole punch cloud. The cloud is below freezing. But water hasn't frozen yet. It forms ice. The water around the ice evaporates. This leaves the hole. Sometimes, rainbows form.

*A hole punch cloud is also called a fallstreak hole.*

# chapter ten

# Raining Animals

**Waterspouts** are whirling towers. They're made of air and water. Some are really violent. They're like tornadoes. They form over land. They move to water. They have heavy winds. They're very strong storms.

Some people think these storms can pick up animals. The storms pick up fish or frogs. They carry them for several miles. They let the animals go. People think it's raining animals. Animals fall from the sky.

Scientists haven't seen this. But many people have reported raining animals.

*Birds and fish can get trapped in the waterspouts.*

One of the first reports was from the first century. A Roman wrote about frog storms. In 1794, French soldiers saw raining toads.

People in Honduras say it rains fish every summer. This happens in a small village. Small silver fish rain down. The people host a party. People in Sri Lanka saw raining fish in 2012. They put fish in buckets. They ate them later. People in the United States have seen raining fish as well. This happened in 1957. It happened in Alabama. Fish, frogs, and crayfish fell from the sky.

Sometimes the animals freeze in the waterspouts. Frozen animals are dangerous. They crash down. They smash windows. They hurt people.

*Some think raining fish is good fortune.*

# Try This!

- Go on a nature walk. Stop and look around. Write a list of all the plants you see. Write a list of all the animals you see.

- Visit a state park. Or visit a national park. Think about why it's important to protect our parks.

- Start a rock collection. Get a book on rocks. Label the rocks.

- Create an organic garden. Read the 45th Parallel Press book on this topic. Take care of your garden. Make a meal. Use food from your garden.

- Visit the ocean. Or visit a pond. Or visit a lake. Touch the water. Draw a picture of it.

# Consider This!

**Take a Position!** Read about global warming. How is nature affected? Is human activity affecting global warming? Argue your point with reasons and evidence.

**Say What?** Many people help nature. Zoologists study animals. Botanists study plants. Geologists study rocks. Research someone who studies nature. Explain what they do.

**Think About It!** Many people are worried about the earth. They think people are ruining our natural resources. Think about ways you can help. What can you do to save the planet?

## Learn More!

- Lewis, J. Patrick, ed. *Book of Nature Poetry: More Than 200 Poems with Photographs That Float, Zoom, and Bloom!* Washington, DC: National Geographic, 2015.
- Mills, Andrea. *Strange But True!* New York: DK, 2015.
- Tornio, Stacy, and Ken Keffer. *The Truth About Nature: A Family's Guide to 144 Common Myths about the Great Outdoors.* Guilford, CT: Falcon Guides, 2014.

# Glossary

**algae (AL-jee)** tiny seaweed

**arid (AR-id)** dry

**bacteria (bak-TEER-ee-uh)** tiny living organisms

**cocoons (kuh-KOONZ)** silky wraps or cases

**compasses (KUHM-puhs-iz)** navigational tools that help people find places

**currents (KUR-uhnts)** water flows

**densely (DENS-lee)** thickly

**dye (DYE)** color

**erosion (ih-ROH-zhuhn)** process of natural forces wearing something down

**evaporation (ih-vap-uh-RAY-shuhn)** water cycle process when liquid turns to gas

**landforms (LAND-formz)** natural features formed on land like mountains and hills

**larvae (LAHR-vee)** worm stage of a fly's life cycle between eggs and adults

**localized (LOH-kuhl-ized)** collected in one place

**monsoons (MAHN-soonz)** heavy rains with winds, storms

**optical (AHP-tih-kuhl)** visual

**pap (PAP)** special koala poop with bacteria

**sap (SAP)** tree or plant juice

**seedlings (SEED-lingz)** baby trees or plants

**survive (sur-VIVE)** to stay alive

**trenches (TRENCH-iz)** long, narrow holes

**waterspouts (WAW-tur-spouts)** whirlwinds over water

**wreckage (REK-uhj)** trash, broken pieces left behind after something is destroyed

# Index